Margaret Edson

WIT

CURRENCY PRESS
The performing arts publisher

First published in Australia in 2020
by Currency Press Pty Ltd,
Gadigal Land, Suite 310, 46–56 Kippax Street, Surry Hills, NSW 2010, Australia
enquiries@currency.com.au
www.currency.com.au

by arrangement with Nick Hern Books, London, and Farrar, Straus and Giroux, New York.

Reprinted 2022, 2023, 2025.

Grateful acknowledgement is made to Harper Collins Publishers for per-mission to reprint an excerpt from *The Runaway Bunny* by Margaret Wise Brown. Copyright ©1942 by Harper Collins Publishers. Text copyright renewed ©1970 by Roberta Brown Rauch. Used by permission of Harper Collins Publishers

The Divine Poems by John Donne, edited by Helen Gardner (second edition, 1978). Reprinted by permission of Oxford University Press. Please apply
to Oxford University Press for permission to use the written version of 'If poysonous mineralls'in any dramatic production or film of *Wit*.

Front cover design by Gabriel Medina; photo by David Barry.
Title logo design by Spot Design.
Typeset by Country Setting, Kingsdown, Kcnt CT14 8ES.
Printed by CanPrint, Canberra, ACT.

Currency Press acknowledges the Traditional Owners of the Country on which we live and work. We pay our respects to all Aboriginal and Torres Strait Islander Elders, past and present.

MARGARET EDSON

Margaret Edson lives in Atlanta, Georgia, where she is an elementary school teacher. Between earning degrees in history and literature, she worked in the cancer and AIDS unit of a research hospital. *Wit*, her first play, won the 1999 Pulitzer Prize for drama.

Wit was first performed at the South Coast Repertory Theater in Costa Mesa, California, on 24 January 1995. It was produced by South Coast Repertory, David Emmes, producing artistic director, and Martin Benson, artistic director. The production was directed by Martin Benson. The set was designed by Cliff Faulkner; the costume design was by Kay Peebles; the lighting design was by Paulie Jenkins; the music and sound design were by Michael Roth. The production manager was Michael Mora. The stage manager was Randall K. Lum. The cast was as follows:

VIVIAN BEARING, PH.D.	Megan Cole
HARVEY KELEKIAN, M.D./MR BEARING.	Richard Doyle
JASON POSNER, M.D.	Brian Drillinger
SUSIE MONAHAN, R.N., B.S.N.	Mary Kay Wulf
E. M. ASHFORD, D.PHIL.	Patricia Fraser
LAB TECHNICIANS/STUDENTS/RESIDENTS.	Christopher Du Val, Kyle Jones, Stacy L. Porter

This text is based on the production of *Wit* that opened at the Union Square Theatre, New York City, on 7 January 1999. It was produced by MCC Theater, Long Wharf Theatre, and Daryl Roth, with Stanley Shopkorn, Robert G. Bartner, and Stanley Kaufelt; associate producer, Lorie Cowen Levy. General management by Roy Gabay. The production was directed by Derek Anson Jones. The set was designed by Myung Hee Cho; the costume design was by Ilona Somogyi; the lighting design was by Michael Chybowski; the music and sound design were by David Van Tieghem; the wigs were by Paul Huntley. The production manager was Kai Brothers. The production stage manager was Katherine Lee Boyer. The casting was by Bernard Telsey Casting. The cast was as follows:

VIVIAN BEARING, PH.D.	Kathleen Chalfant
HARVEY KELEKIAN, M.D./MR BEARING.	Walter Charles
JASON POSNER, M.D.	Alec Phoenix
SUSIE MONAHAN, R.N., B.S.N.	Paula Pizzi
E. M. ASHFORD, D.PHIL.	Helen Stenborg
LAB TECHNICIANS/STUDENTS/RESIDENTS.	Brian J. Carter, Daniel Sarnelli, Alli Steinberg, Lisa Tharps

The production opened originally at the Long Wharf Theatre, New Haven, Connecticut, on 31 October 1997. Doug Hughes, artistic director; Michael Ross, managing director.

It opened in New York at MCC Theater, 17 September 1998. Robert LuPone and Bernard Telsey, executive directors; William Cantler, associate director.

Wit opened at the Vaudeville Theatre, London, on 3 April 2000, with Kathleen Chalfant as Vivian Bearing, directed by Leigh Silverman (recreating the original New York production).

Notes

Most of the action, but not all, takes place in a room of the University Hospital Comprehensive Cancer Centre. The stage is empty, and furniture is rolled on and off by the technicians.

Jason and Kelekian wear lab coats, but each has a different shirt and tie every time he enters. Susie wears white jeans, white sneakers, and a different blouse each entrance.

Scenes are indicated by a three-line space in the script; there is no break in the action between scenes, but there might be a change in lighting. There is no intermission.

Vivian has a central-venous-access catheter over her left breast, so the IV tubing goes there, not into her arm. The IV pole, with a Port-a-Pump attached, rolls easily on wheels. Every time the IV pole reappears, it has a different configuration of bottles.

Acknowledgements

Thanks to the cast that read the first draft of *Wit* in July 1991: Joyce Edson, Derek Anson Jones, Michael Edson, Leslie Spitz-Edson, and Calvin Gidney. Thanks to Mary and Steve Ales and the late Ruth Mortimer for reading the next draft. Thanks to Jerry Patch, Martin Benson, and my friends at South Coast Repertory. Thanks to Doug Hughes and my friends at Long Wharf Theatre, and Bernard Telsey and my friends at MCC. Thanks to Carolyn French and my friends at the Fifi Oscard Agency. Thanks to Linda Merrill for hearing every word.

Characters

VIVIAN BEARING, PH.D.
50; professor of seventeenth-century poetry at the university

HARVEY KELEKIAN, M.D.
50; chief of medical oncology, University Hospital

JASON POSNER, M.D.
28; clinical fellow, Medical Oncology Branch

SUSIE MONAHAN, R.N., B.S.N.
28; primary nurse, Cancer Inpatient Unit

E. M. ASHFORD, D.PHIL.
80; professor emerita of English literature

MR BEARING
Vivian's father

LAB TECHNICIANS
CLINICAL FELLOWS
STUDENTS
CODE TEAM

The play may be performed with a cast of nine: the four TECHNICIANS, FELLOWS, STUDENTS, *and* CODE TEAM MEMBERS *should double;* DR KELEKIAN *and* MR BEARING *should double.*

VIVIAN BEARING *walks on the empty stage pushing her IV pole. She is fifty, tall and very thin, barefoot, and completely bald. She wears two hospital gowns – one tied in the front and one tied in the back – a baseball cap, and a hospital ID bracelet. The house lights are at half strength.* VIVIAN *looks out at the audience, sizing them up.*

VIVIAN (*in false familiarity, waving and nodding to the audience*). Hi. How are you feeling today? Great. That's just great. (*In her own professorial tone.*) This is not my standard greeting, I assure you.

I tend toward something a little more formal, a little less inquisitive, such as, say, 'Hello.'

But it is the standard greeting here.

There is some debate as to the correct response to this salutation. Should one reply 'I feel good,' using 'feel' as a copulative to link the subject, 'I,' to its subjective complement, 'good'; or 'I feel well,' modifying with an adverb the subject's state of being?

I don't know. I am a professor of seventeenth-century poetry, specialising in the Holy Sonnets of John Donne.

So I just say, 'Fine.'

Of course it is not very often that I do feel fine.

I have been asked 'How are you feeling today?' while I was throwing up into a plastic washbasin. I have been asked as I was emerging from a four-hour operation with a tube in every orifice, 'How are you feeling today?'

I am waiting for the moment when someone asks me this question and I am dead.

I'm a little sorry I'll miss that.

It is unfortunate that this remarkable line of inquiry has come to me so late in my career. I could have exploited its feigned solicitude to great advantage: as I was distributing the final examination to the graduate course in seventeenth-century textual criticism – 'Hi. How are you feeling today?'

Of course I would not be wearing this costume at the time, so the question's *ironic significance* would not be fully apparent.

As I trust it is now.

Irony is a literary device that will necessarily be deployed to great effect.

I ardently wish this were not so. I would prefer that a play about me be cast in the mythic-heroic-pastoral mode; but the facts, most notably stage-four metastatic ovarian cancer, conspire against that. *The Faerie Queene* this is not.

And I was dismayed to discover that the play would contain elements of . . . *humour.*

I have been, at best, an *unwitting* accomplice. (*She pauses.*) It is not my intention to give away the plot; but I think I die at the end.

They've given me less than two hours.

If I were poetically inclined, I might employ a threadbare metaphor – the sands of time slipping through the hour-glass, the two-hour glass.

> Now our sands are almost run;
> More a little, and then dumb.

Shakespeare. I trust the name is familiar.

At the moment, however, I am disinclined to poetry.

I've got less than two hours. Then: curtain.

She disconnects herself from the IV pole and shoves it to a crossing TECHNICIAN. *The house lights go out.*

VIVIAN. I'll never forget the time I found out I had cancer.

DR HARVEY KELEKIAN *enters at a big desk piled high with papers.*

KELEKIAN. You have cancer.

VIVIAN (*to audience*). See? Unforgettable. It was something of a shock. I had to sit down. (*She plops down.*)

KELEKIAN. Please sit down. Miss Bearing, you have advanced metastatic ovarian cancer.

VIVIAN. Go on.

KELEKIAN. You are a professor, Miss Bearing.

VIVIAN. Like yourself, Dr Kelekian.

KELEKIAN. Well, yes. Now then. You present with a growth that, unfortunately, went undetected in stages one, two, and three. Now it is an insidious adenocarcinoma, which has spread from the primary adnexal mass –

VIVIAN. 'Insidious'?

KELEKIAN. 'Insidious' means undetectable at an –

VIVIAN. 'Insidious' *means* treacherous.

KELEKIAN. Shall I continue?

VIVIAN. By all means.

KELEKIAN. Good. In invasive epithelial carcinoma, the most effective treatment modality is a chemotherapeutic agent. We are developing an experimental combination of drugs designed	VIVIAN: Insidious. Hmm. Curious word choice. Cancer. Cancel.
for primary-site ovarian, with a target specificity of stage three-and-- beyond administration.	'By cancer nature's changing course untrimmed.' No – that's not it.
Am I going too fast?	(*To* KELEKIAN.) No.

Good.

You will be hospitalised as an in-patient for treatment each cycle. You will be on complete intake-and-output measurement for three days after each treatment to monitor kidney function. After the initial eight cycles, you will have another battery of tests.

The antineoplastic will inevitably affect some healthy cells, including those lining the gastro-intestinal tract from the lips to the anus, and the hair follicles. We will of course be relying on your resolve to with-stand some of the more pernicious side effects.

Must read something about cancer.

Must get some books, articles. Assemble a bibliography.

Is anyone doing research on cancer?

Concentrate.

Antineoplastic, Anti: against. Neo: new. Plastic. To mould. Shaping. Antineoplastic. Against new shaping.

Hair follicles. My resolve.

'Pernicious.' That doesn't seem –

KELEKIAN. Miss Bearing?

VIVIAN. I beg your pardon?

KELEKIAN. Do you have any questions so far?

VIVIAN. Please, go on.

KELEKIAN. Perhaps some of these terms are new. I realise –

VIVIAN. No, no. Ah. You're being very thorough.

KELEKIAN. I make a point of it. And I always emphasise it with my students –

VIVIAN. So do I. 'Thoroughness' – I always tell my students, but they are constitutionally averse to painstaking work.

KELEKIAN. Yours, too.

VIVIAN. Oh, it's worse every year.

KELEKIAN. And this is not dermatology, it's medical oncology, for Chrissake.

VIVIAN. My students read through a text once – *once*! – and think it's time for a break.

KELEKIAN. Mine are blind.

VIVIAN. Well, mine are deaf.

KELEKIAN (*resigned, but warmly*). You just have to hope . . .

VIVIAN (*not so sure*). I suppose.

Pause.

KELEKIAN. Where were we, Dr Bearing?

VIVIAN. I believe I was being thoroughly diagnosed.

KELEKIAN. Right. Now. The tumour is spreading very quickly, and this treatment is very aggressive. So far, so good?

VIVIAN. Yes.

KELEKIAN. Better not teach next semester.

VIVIAN (*indignant*). Out of the question.

KELEKIAN. The first week of each cycle you'll be hospitalised for chemotherapy; the next week you may feel a little tired; the next two weeks'll be fine, relatively. This cycle will repeat eight times, as I said before.

VIVIAN. Eight months like that?

KELEKIAN. This treatment is the strongest thing we have to offer you. And, as research, it will make a significant contribution to our knowledge.

VIVIAN. Knowledge, yes.

KELEKIAN (*giving her a piece of paper*). Here is the informed-consent form. Should you agree, you sign there, at the bottom. Is there a family member you want me to explain this to?

VIVIAN (*signing*). That won't be necessary.

KELEKIAN (*taking back the paper*). Good. The important thing is for you to take the full dose of chemotherapy. There may be times when you'll wish for a lesser dose, due to the side effects. But we've got to go full-force. The experimental phase has got to have the maximum dose to be of any use. Dr Bearing –

VIVIAN. Yes?

KELEKIAN. You must be very tough. Do you think you can be very tough?

VIVIAN. You needn't worry.

KELEKIAN. Good. Excellent.

KELEKIAN *and the desk exit as* VIVIAN *stands and walks forward.*

VIVIAN (*hesitantly*). I should have asked more questions, because I know there's going to be a test.

I have cancer, insidious cancer, with pernicious side effects – no, the *treatment* has pernicious side effects.

I have stage-four metastatic ovarian cancer. There is no stage five. Oh, and I have to be very tough. It appears to be a matter, as the saying goes, of life and death.

I know all about life and death. I am, after all, a scholar of Donne's Holy Sonnets, which explore mortality in greater depth than any other body of work in the English language.

And I know for a fact that I am tough. A demanding professor. Uncompromising. Never one to turn from a challenge. That is why I chose, while a student of the great E.M. Ashford, to study Donne.

PROFESSOR E.M. ASHFORD, *fifty-two, enters, seated at the same desk as* KELEKIAN *was. The scene is twenty-eight years ago.* VIVIAN *suddenly turns twenty-two, eager and intimidated.*

VIVIAN. Professor Ashford?

E.M. Do it again.

VIVIAN (*to audience*). It was something of a shock. I had to sit down. (*She plops down.*)

E.M. Please sit down. Your essay on Holy Sonnet Six, Miss Bearing, is a melodrama, with a veneer of scholarship unworthy of you – to say nothing of Donne. Do it again.

VIVIAN. I, ah . . .

E.M. You must begin with a text, Miss Bearing, not with a feeling.

> Death be not proud, though some have called thee
> Mighty and dreadfull, for, thou art not soe.

You have entirely missed the point of the poem, because, I must tell you, you have used an edition of the text that is inauthentically punctuated. In the Gardner edition –

VIVIAN. That edition was checked out of the library –

E.M. Miss Bearing!

VIVIAN. Sorry.

E.M. You take this too lightly, Miss Bearing. This is Metaphysical Poetry, not The Modern Novel. The standards of scholarship and critical reading which one would apply to any other text are simply insufficient. The effort must be total for the results to be meaningful. Do you think the punctuation of the last line of this sonnet is merely an insignificant detail?

The sonnet begins with a valiant struggle with death, calling on all the forces of intellect and drama to vanquish the enemy. But it is ultimately about overcoming the seemingly insuperable barriers separating life, death, and eternal life.

In the edition you chose, this profoundly simple meaning is sacrificed to hysterical punctuation:

> And Death – *capital D* – shall be no more – *semi-colon!*
> Death – *capital D* – *comma* – thou shalt die – *exclamation point!*

If you go in for this sort of thing, I suggest you take up Shakespeare.

Gardner's edition of the Holy Sonnets returns to the Westmoreland manuscript source of 1610 – not for sentimental reasons, I assure you, but because Helen Gardner is a *scholar.* It reads:

And death shall be no more, *comma*, Death thou shalt die.

As she recites this line, she makes a little gesture at the comma.

Nothing but a breath – a comma – separates life from life everlasting. It is very simple really. With the original punctuation restored, death is no longer something to act out on a stage, with exclamation points. It's a comma, a pause.

This way, the *uncompromising* way, one learns something from this poem, wouldn't you say? Life, death. Soul, God. Past, present. Not insuperable barriers, not semicolons, just a comma.

VIVIAN. Life, death . . . I see. (*Standing.*) It's a metaphysical conceit. It's wit! I'll go back to the library and rewrite the paper –

E.M. (*standing, emphatically*). It is *not wit*, Miss Bearing. It is truth. (*Walking around the desk to her.*) The paper's not the point.

VIVIAN. It isn't?

E.M. (*tenderly*). Vivian. You're a bright young woman. Use your intelligence. Don't go back to the library. Go out. Enjoy yourself with your friends. Hmm?

VIVIAN *walks away.* E.M. *slides off.*

VIVIAN (*as she gradually returns to the hospital*). I, ah, went outside. The sun was very bright. I, ah, walked around, past the . . . There were students on the lawn, talking about nothing, laughing. The insuperable barrier between one thing and another is . . . just a comma? Simple human truth, uncompromising scholarly standards? They're *connected?*

I just couldn't . . .

I went back to the library.

Anyway.

All right. Significant contribution to knowledge.

Eight cycles of chemotherapy. Give me the full dose, the full dose every time.

In a burst of activity, the hospital scene is created.

VIVIAN. The attention was flattering. For the first five minutes. Now I know how poems feel.

SUSIE MONAHAN, VIVIAN*'s primary nurse, gives* VIVIAN *her chart, then puts her in a wheelchair and takes her to her first appointment: chest x-ray. This and all other diagnostic tests are suggested by light and sound.*

TECHNICIAN 1. Name.

VIVIAN. My name? Vivian Bearing.

TECHNICIAN 1. Huh?

VIVIAN. Bearing. B-E-A-R-I-N-G. Vivian. V–I-V-I-A-N.

TECHNICIAN 1. Doctor.

VIVIAN. Yes, I have a Ph.D.

TECHNICIAN 1. *Your* doctor.

VIVIAN. Oh. Dr Harvey Kelekian.

TECHNICIAN 1 *positions her so that she is leaning forward and embracing the metal plate, then steps offstage.*

VIVIAN. *I* am a doctor of philosophy –

TECHNICIAN 1 (*from offstage*). Take a deep breath, and hold it. (*Pause, with light and sound.*) Okay.

VIVIAN. – a scholar of seventeenth-century poetry.

TECHNICIAN 1 (*from offstage*) Turn sideways, arms behind your head, and hold it. (*Pause.*) Okay.

VIVIAN. I have made an immeasurable contribution to the discipline of English literature. (TECHNICIAN 1 *returns and puts her in the wheelchair.*) I am, in short, a force.

TECHNICIAN 1 *rolls her to upper GI series, where* TECHNICIAN 2 *picks up.*

TECHNICIAN 2. Name.

VIVIAN. Lucy, Countess of Bedford.

TECHNICIAN 2 (*checking a printout*). I don't see it here.

VIVIAN. My name is Vivian Bearing. B-E-A-R-I-N-G. Dr Kelekian is my doctor.

TECHNICIAN 2. Okay. Lie down. (TECHNICIAN 2 *positions her on a stretcher and leaves. Light and sound suggest the filming.*)

VIVIAN. After an outstanding undergraduate career, I studied with Professor E. M. Ashford for three years, during which time I learned by instruction and example what it means to be a scholar of distinction.

As her research fellow, my principal task was the alphabetising of index cards for Ashford's monumental critical edition of Donne's *Devotions upon Emergent Occasions.*

During the procedure, another TECHNICIAN *takes the wheelchair away.*

I am thanked in the preface: 'Miss Vivian Bearing for her able assistance.'

My dissertation, 'Ejaculations in Seventeenth-Century Manuscript and Printed Editions of the Holy Sonnets: a Comparison,' was revised for publication in the *Journal of English Texts,* a very prestigious venue for a first appearance.

TECHNICIAN 2. Where's your wheelchair?

VIVIAN. I do not know. I was busy just now.

TECHNICIAN 2. Well, how are you going to get out of here?

VIVIAN. Well, I do not know. Perhaps you would like me to stay.

TECHNICIAN 2. I guess I got to go find you a chair.

VIVIAN (*sarcastically*). Don't inconvenience yourself on my behalf.

TECHNICIAN 2 *leaves to get a wheelchair.*

My second article, a classic explication of Donne's sonnet 'Death be not proud,' was published in *Critical Discourse.*

The success of the essay prompted the University Press to solicit a volume on the twelve Holy Sonnets in the 1633 edition, which I produced in the remarkably short span of three years. My book, entitled *Made Cunningly,* remains an immense success, in paper as well as cloth.

In it, I devote one chapter to a thorough examination of each sonnet, discussing every word in extensive detail.

TECHNICIAN 2 *returns with a wheelchair.*

TECHNICIAN 2. Here.

VIVIAN. I summarise previous critical interpretations of the text and offer my own analysis. It is exhaustive.

TECHNICIAN 2 *deposits her at CT scan.*

Bearing. B-E-A-R-I-N-G. Kelekian.

TECHNICIAN 3 *has* VIVIAN *lie down on a metal stretcher. Light and sound suggest the procedure.*

TECHNICIAN 3. Here. Hold still.

VIVIAN. For how long?

TECHNICIAN 3. Just a little while. (TECHNICIAN 3 *leaves. Silence.*)

VIVIAN. The scholarly study of poetic texts requires a capacity for scrupulously detailed examination, particularly the poetry of John Donne.

The salient characteristic of the poems is wit: 'Itchy outbreaks of far-fetched wit,' as Donne himself said.

To the common reader – that is to say, the undergraduate with a B-plus or better average – wit provides an invaluable exercise for sharpening the mental faculties, for stimulating the flash of comprehension that can only follow hours of exacting and seemingly pointless scrutiny.

TECHNICIAN 3 *puts* VIVIAN *back in the wheelchair and wheels her toward the unit. Partway,* TECHNICIAN 3 *gives the chair a shove and* SUSIE MONAHAN, VIVIAN*'s primary nurse, takes over.* SUSIE *rolls* VIVIAN *to the exam room.*

To the scholar, to the mind comprehensively trained in the subtleties of seventeenth-century vocabulary, versification, and theological, historical, geographical, political, and mythological allusions, Donne's wit is . . . a way to see how good you really are.

After twenty years, I can say with confidence, no one is quite as good as I.

By now, SUSIE *has helped* VIVIAN *sit on the exam table.* DR JASON POSNER, *clinical fellow, stands in the doorway.*

JASON. Ah, Susie?

SUSIE. Oh, hi.

JASON. Ready when you are.

SUSIE. Okay. Go ahead. Ms Bearing, this is Jason Posner. He's going to do your history, ask you a bunch of questions. He's Dr Kelekian's fellow.

SUSIE *is busy in the room, setting up for the exam.*

JASON. Hi, Professor Bearing. I'm Dr Posner, clinical fellow in the medical oncology branch, working with Dr Kelekian.

Professor Bearing, I, ah, I was an undergraduate at the U. I took your course in seventeenth-century poetry.

VIVIAN. You did?

JASON. Yes. I thought it was excellent.

VIVIAN. Thank you. Were you an English major?

JASON. No. Biochemistry. But you can't get into medical school unless you're well-rounded. And I made a bet with myself that I could get an A in the three hardest courses on campus.

SUSIE. Howdjya, do, Jace?

JASON. Success.

VIVIAN (*doubtful*). Really?

JASON. A minus. It was a very tough course. (*To* SUSIE.) I'll call you.

SUSIE. Okay. (*She leaves.*)

JASON. I'll just pull this over. (*He gets a little stool on wheels.*) Get the proxemics right here. There. (*Nervously.*) Good. Now. I'm going to be taking your history. It's a medical interview, and then I give you an exam.

VIVIAN. I believe Dr Kelekian has already done that.

JASON. Well, I know, but Dr Kelekian wants *me* to do it, too. Now. I'll be taking a few notes as we go along.

VIVIAN. Very well.

JASON. Okay. Let's get started. How are you feeling today?

VIVIAN. Fine, thank you.

JASON. Good. How is your general health?

VIVIAN. Fine.

JASON. Excellent. Okay. We know you are an academic.

VIVIAN. Yes, we've established that.

JASON. So we don't need to talk about your interesting work.

VIVIAN. No.

The following questions and answers go extremely quickly.

JASON. How old are you?

VIVIAN. Fifty.

JASON. Are you married?

VIVIAN. No.

JASON. Are your parents living?

VIVIAN. No.

JASON. How and when did they die?

VIVIAN. My father, suddenly, when I was twenty, of a heart attack. My mother, slowly, when I was forty-one and forty-two, of cancer. Breast cancer.

JASON. Cancer?

VIVIAN. Breast cancer.

JASON. I see. Any siblings?

VIVIAN. No.

JASON. Do you have any questions so far?

VIVIAN. Not so far.

JASON. Well, that about does it for your life history.

VIVIAN. Yes, that's all there is to my life history.

JASON. Now I'm going to ask you about your past medical history. Have you ever been hospitalised?

VIVIAN. I had my tonsils out when I was eight.

JASON. Have you ever been pregnant?

VIVIAN. No.

JASON. Ever had heart murmurs? High blood pressure?

VIVIAN. No.

JASON. Stomach, liver, kidney problems?

VIVIAN. No.

JASON. Venereal diseases? Uterine infections?

VIVIAN. No.

JASON. Thyroid, diabetes, cancer?

VIVIAN. No – cancer, yes.

JASON. When?

VIVIAN. Now.

JASON. Well, not including now.

VIVIAN. In that case, no.

JASON. Okay. Clinical depression? Nervous breakdowns? Suicide attempts?

VIVIAN. No.

JASON. Do you smoke?

VIVIAN. No.

JASON. Ethanol?

VIVIAN. I'm sorry?

JASON. Alcohol.

VIVIAN. Oh. Ethanol. Yes, I drink wine.

JASON. How much? How often?

VIVIAN. A glass with dinner occasionally. And perhaps a Scotch every now and then.

JASON. Do you use substances?

VIVIAN. Such as.

JASON. Marijuana, cocaine, crack cocaine, PCP, ecstasy, poppers –

VIVIAN. No.

JASON. Do you drink caffeinated beverages?

VIVIAN. Oh, yes!

JASON. Which ones?

VIVIAN. Coffee. A few cups a day.

JASON. How many?

VIVIAN. Two . . . to six. But I really don't think that's immoderate –

JASON. How often do you undergo routine medical check-ups?

VIVIAN. Well, not as often as I should, probably, but I've felt fine, I really have.

JASON. So the answer is?

VIVIAN. Every three to . . . five years.

JASON. What do you do for exercise?

VIVIAN. Pace.

JASON. Are you having sexual relations?

VIVIAN. Not at the moment.

JASON. Are you pre- or post-menopausal?

VIVIAN. Pre.

JASON. When was the first day of your last period?

VIVIAN. Ah, ten days – two weeks ago.

JASON. Okay. When did you first notice your present complaint?

VIVIAN. This time, now?

JASON. Yes.

VIVIAN. Oh, about four months ago. I felt a pain in my stomach, in my abdomen, like a cramp, but not the same.

JASON. How did it feel?

VIVIAN. Like a cramp.

JASON. But not the same?

VIVIAN. No, duller, and stronger. I can't describe it.

JASON. What came next?

VIVIAN. Well, I just, I don't know, I started noticing my body, little things. I would be teaching, and feel a sharp pain.

JASON. What kind of pain?

VIVIAN. Sharp, and sudden. Then it would go away. Or I would be tired. Exhausted. I was working on a major project, the article on John Donne for *The Oxford Encyclopedia of English Literature.* It was a great honour. But I had a very strict deadline.

JASON. So you would say you were under stress?

VIVIAN. It wasn't so much more stress than usual, I just couldn't withstand it this time. I don't know.

JASON. So?

VIVIAN. So I went to Dr Chin, my gynaecologist, after I had turned in the article, and explained all this. She examined me, and sent me to Jefferson the internist, and he sent me to Kelekian because he thought I might have a tumour.

JASON. And that's it?

VIVIAN. Till now.

JASON. Hmmm. Well, that's very interesting.

Nervous pause.

Well, I guess I'll start the examination. It'll only take a few minutes. Why don't you, um, sort of lie back, and – oh – relax.

He helps her lie back on the table, raises the stirrups out of the table, raises her legs and puts them in the stirrups, and puts a paper sheet over her.

Be very relaxed. This won't hurt. Let me get this sheet. Okay. Just stay calm. Okay. Put your feet in these stirrups. Okay. Just. There. Okay? Now. Oh, I have to go get Susie. Got to have a girl here. Some crazy clinical rule. Um. I'll be right back. Don't move.

JASON *leaves. Long pause. He is seen walking quickly back and forth in the hall and calling* SUSIE*'s name as he goes by.*

VIVIAN (*to herself*). I wish I had given him an A. (*Silence.*)

Two times one is two.
Two times two is four.
Two times three is six.
Um.
Oh.

> Death be not proud, though some have called thee
> Mighty and dreadfull, for, thou art not soe,
> For, those, whom thou think'st, thou dost overthrow,
> Die not, poore death, nor yet canst thou kill mee . . .

JASON (*in the hallway*). Has anybody seen Susie?

VIVIAN (*losing her place for a second*). Ah.

> Thou'art slave to Fate, chance, kings, and desperate men,
> And dost with poyson, warre, and sicknesse dwell,
> And poppie, 'or charmes can make us sleepe as well,
> And better than thy stroake; why swell'st thou then?

JASON (*in the hallway*). She was here just a minute ago.

VIVIAN.
> One short sleepe past, wee wake eternally,
> And death shall be no more – *comma* – Death thou shalt die.

JASON *and* SUSIE *return.*

JASON. Okay. Here's everything. Okay.

SUSIE. What is this? Why did you leave her?

JASON (*to* SUSIE). I had to find you. Now, come on. (*To* VIVIAN.) We're ready, Professor Bearing. (*To himself, as he puts on exam gloves.*) Get these on. Okay. Just lift this up. Ooh. Okay. (*As much to himself as to her.*) Just relax. (*He begins the pelvic exam, with one hand on her abdomen and the other inside her, looking blankly at the ceiling as he feels around.*) Okay. (*Silence.*) Susie, isn't that interesting, that I had Professor Bearing.

SUSIE. Yeah. I wish I had taken some literature. I don't know anything about poetry.

JASON (*trying to be casual*). Professor Bearing was very

highly regarded on campus. It looked very good on my transcript that I had taken her course. (*Silence.*) They even asked me about it in my interview for med school – (*He feels the mass and does a double take.*) Jesus! (*Tense silence. He is amazed and fascinated.*)

SUSIE. What?

VIVIAN. What?

JASON. Um. (*He tries for composure.*) Yeah. I survived Bearing's course. No problem. Heh. (*Silence.*) Yeah, John Donne, those metaphysical poets, that metaphysical wit. Hardest poetry in the English department. Like to see *them* try biochemistry. (*Silence.*) Okay. We're about done. Okay. That's it. Okay, Professor Bearing. Let's take your feet out, there. (*He takes off his gloves and throws them away.*) Okay. I gotta go. I gotta go.

JASON *quickly leaves.* VIVIAN *slowly gets up from this scene and walks stiffly away.* SUSIE *cleans up the exam room and exits.*

VIVIAN (*walking downstage to audience*). That . . . was . . . hard. That . . . was . . .

One thing can be said for an eight-month course of cancer treatment: it is highly educational. I am learning to suffer.

Yes, it is mildly uncomfortable to have an electrocardiogram, but the . . . agony . . . of a proctosigmoidoscopy sweeps it from memory. Yes, it was embarrassing to have to wear a nightgown all day long – two nightgowns! – but that seemed like a positive privilege compared to watching myself go bald. Yes, having a former student give me a pelvic exam was thoroughly *degrading* – and I use the term deliberately – but I could not have imagined the depths of humiliation that –

Oh, God – (VIVIAN *runs across the stage to her hospital room, dives onto the bed, and throws up into a large plastic washbasin.*) Oh, God. Oh. Oh. (*She lies slumped on the bed, fastened to the IV, which now includes a small bottle with a bright orange label.*) Oh, God. It can't be. (*Silence.*) Oh,

God. Please. Steady. Steady. (*Silence.*) Oh – Oh, no! (*She throws up again, moans, and retches in agony.*) Oh, God. What's left? I haven't eaten in two days. What's left to puke?

You may remark that my vocabulary has taken a turn for the Anglo-Saxon.

God, I'm going to barf my brains out.

(*She begins to relax.*) If I actually did barf my brains out, it would be a great loss to my discipline. Of course, not a few of my colleagues would be relieved. To say nothing of my students.

It's not that I'm controversial. Just uncompromising. Ooh – (*She lunges for the basin. Nothing.*) Oh. (*Silence.*) False alarm. If the word went round that Vivian Bearing had barfed her brains out . . .

Well, first my colleagues, most of whom are my former students, would scramble madly for my position. Then their consciences would flare up, so to honour *my* memory they would put together a collection of *their* essays about John Donne. The volume would begin with a warm introduction, capturing my most endearing qualities. It would be short. But sweet.

Published *and* perished.

Now, watch this. I have to ring the bell (*She presses the button on the bed.*) to get someone to come and measure this emesis, and record the amount on a chart of my intake and output. This counts as output.

SUSIE *enters.*

SUSIE (*brightly*). How you doing, Ms Bearing? You having some nausea?

VIVIAN (*weakly*). Uhh, yes.

SUSIE. Why don't I take that? Here.

VIVIAN. It's about 300 cc's.

SUSIE. That all?

VIVIAN. It was very hard work.

SUSIE *takes the basin to the bathroom and rinses it.*

SUSIE. Yup. Three hundred. Good guess. (*She marks the graph.*) Okay. Anything else I can get for you? Some Jell-O or anything?

VIVIAN. Thank you, no.

SUSIE. You okay all by yourself here?

VIVIAN. Yes.

SUSIE. You're not having a lot of visitors, are you?

VIVIAN (*correcting*). None, to be precise.

SUSIE. Yeah, I didn't think so. Is there somebody you want me to call for you?

VIVIAN. That won't be necessary.

SUSIE. Well, I'll just pop my head in every once in a while to see how you're coming along. Kelekian and the fellows should be in soon. (*She touches* VIVIAN*'s arm.*) If there's anything you need, you just ring.

VIVIAN (*uncomfortable with kindness*). Thank you.

SUSIE. Okay. Just call. (SUSIE *disconnects the IV bottle with the orange label and takes it with her as she leaves.* VIVIAN *lies still. Silence.*)

VIVIAN. In this dramatic structure you will see the most interesting aspects of my tenure as an in-patient receiving experimental chemotherapy for advanced metastatic ovarian cancer.

But as I am a *scholar* before . . . an impresario, I feel obliged to document what it is like here most of the time, between the dramatic climaxes. Between the spectacles.

In truth, it is like this:

She ceremoniously lies back and stares at the ceiling.

You cannot imagine how time . . . can be . . . so still.

It hangs. It weighs. And yet there is so little of it.
It goes so slowly, and yet it is so scarce.

If I were writing this scene, it would last a full fifteen minutes. I would lie here, and you would sit there.

She looks at the audience, daring them.

Not to worry. Brevity is the soul of wit. But if you think eight months of cancer treatment is tedious for the *audience,* consider how it feels to play my part.

All right. All right. It is Friday morning: Grand Rounds. (*Loudly, giving a cue.*) Action.

KELEKIAN *enters, followed by* JASON *and four other* FELLOWS.

KELEKIAN. Dr Bearing.

VIVIAN. Dr Kelekian.

KELEKIAN. Jason. (JASON *moves to the front of the group.*)

JASON. Professor Bearing. How are you feeling today?

VIVIAN. Fine.

JASON. That's great. That's just great. (*He takes a sheet and carefully covers her legs and groin, then pulls up her gown to reveal her entire abdomen. He is barely audible, but his gestures are clear.*)

VIVIAN. 'Grand Rounds.' The term is theirs. Not 'Grand' in the traditional sense of sweeping or magnificent. Not 'Rounds' as in a musical canon, or a *round* of applause (though either would be refreshing at this point). Here, 'Rounds' seems to signify darting *around* the main

JASON: Very late detection. Staged as a four upon admission. Hexamethophosphacil with Vinplatin to potentiate. Hex at 300 mg. per meter squared, Vin at 100. Today is cycle two, day three. Both cycles at the *full dose.* (*The* FELLOWS *are impressed.*)

issue . . . which I suppose would be the struggle for life . . . *my* life . . . with heated discussions of side effects, other complaints, additional treatments.

Grand Rounds is not Grand Opera. But compared to lying here, it is positively *dramatic*.

Full of subservience, hierarchy, gratuitous displays, sublimated rivalries – I feel right at home. It is just like a graduate seminar.

With one important difference: in Grand Rounds, *they* read *me* like a book. Once I did the teaching, now I am taught.

This is much easier. I just hold still and look cancerous. It requires less acting every time.

Excellent command of details.

The primary site is – *here* (*He puts his finger on the spot on her abdomen.*), behind the left ovary. Metastases are suspected in the peritoneal cavity here. And – here. (*He touches those spots.*)

Full lymphatic involvement. (*He moves his hands over her entire body.*)

At the time of first-look surgery, a significant part of the tumour was de-bulked, mostly in this area – *here.* (*He points to each organ, poking her abdomen.*) Left, right ovaries. Fallopian tubes. Uterus. All out.

Evidence of primary-site shrinkage. Shrinking in metastatic tumours has not been documented. Primary mass frankly palpable in pelvic exam, frankly, all through here – *here*. (*Some* FELLOWS *reach and press where he is pointing.*)

KELEKIAN. Excellent command of details.

VIVIAN (*to herself*). I taught him, you know –

KELEKIAN. Okay. Problem areas with Hex and Vin. (*He addresses all the* FELLOWS, *but* JASON *answers first and they resent him.*)

FELLOW 1. Myelosu –

JASON (*interrupting*). Well, first of course is myelosuppression, a lowering of blood-cell counts. It goes without saying. With this combination of agents, nephrotoxicity will be next.

KELEKIAN. Go on.

JASON. The kidneys are designed to filter out impurities in the bloodstream. In trying to filter the chemotherapeutic agent out of the bloodstream, the kidneys shut down.

KELEKIAN. Intervention.

JASON. Hydration.

KELEKIAN. Monitoring.

JASON. Full recording of fluid intake and output, as you see here on these graphs, to monitor hydration and kidney function. Totals monitored daily by the clinical fellow, as per the protocol.

KELEKIAN. Anybody else. Side effects.

FELLOW 1. Nausea and vomiting.

KELEKIAN. Jason.

JASON. Routine.

FELLOW 2. Pain while urinating.

JASON. Routine. (*The* FELLOWS *are trying to catch* JASON.)

FELLOW 3. Psychological depression.

JASON. No way.

The FELLOWS *are silent.*

KELEKIAN (*standing by* VIVIAN *at the head of the bed*). Anything else. Other complaints with Hexamethophosphacil and Vinplatin. Come on. (*Silence.* KELEKIAN *and* VIVIAN *wait together for the correct answer.*)

FELLOW 4. Mouth sores.

JASON. Not yet.

FELLOW 2 (*timidly*). Skin rash?

JASON. Nope.

KELEKIAN (*sharing this with* VIVIAN). Why do we waste our time, Dr Bearing?

VIVIAN (*delighted*). I do not know, Dr Kelekian.

KELEKIAN (*to the* FELLOWS). Use your eyes. (*All* FELLOWS *look closely at* VIVIAN.) Jesus God. Hair loss.

FELLOWS (*all protesting.* VIVIAN *and* KELEKIAN *are amused*).

– Come on.

– You can see it.

– It doesn't count.

– No fair.

KELEKIAN. Jason.

JASON (*begrudgingly*). Hair loss after first cycle of treatment.

KELEKIAN. That's better. (*To* VIVIAN.) Dr Bearing. Full dose. Excellent. Keep pushing the fluids.

The FELLOWS *leave.* KELEKIAN *stops* JASON.

KELEKIAN. Jason.

JASON. Huh?

KELEKIAN. Clinical.

JASON. Oh, right. (*To* VIVIAN.) Thank you, Professor Bearing. You've been very co-operative. (*They leave her with her stomach uncovered.*)

VIVIAN. Wasn't that . . . Grand? (*She gets up without the IV pole.*) At times, this obsessively detailed examination, this *scrutiny* seems to me to be a nefarious business. On the other hand, what is the alternative? Ignorance? Ignorance may be . . . bliss; but it is not a very noble goal.

So I play my part.

Pause.

I receive chemotherapy, throw up, am subjected to countless indignities, feel better, go home. Eight cycles. Eight neat little strophes. Oh, there have been the usual variations, subplots, red herrings: hepatotoxicity (liver poison), neuropathy (nerve death).

(*Righteously.*) They are medical terms. I look them up.

It has always been my custom to treat words with respect.

I can recall the time – the very hour of the very day – when I knew words would be my life's work.

A pile of six little white books appears, with MR BEARING, VIVIAN*'s father, seated behind an open newspaper.*

It was my fifth birthday.

VIVIAN, *now a child, flops down to the books.*

I liked that one best.

MR BEARING (*disinterested but tolerant, never distracted from his newspaper*). Read another.

VIVIAN. I think I'll read . . . (*She takes a book from the stack and reads its spine intently.*) *The Tale of the Flopsy Bunnies.* (*Reading the front cover.*) *The Tale of the Flopsy Bunnies.* It has little bunnies on the front.

(*Opening to the title page.*) *The Tale of the Flopsy Bunnies* by Beatrix Potter. (*She turns the page and begins to read.*)

It is said that the effect of eating too much lettuce is sopor – sop – or – what is that word?

MR BEARING. Sound it out.

VIVIAN. Sop – or – fic. Sop – or – i – fic. Soporific. What does that mean?

MR BEARING. Soporific. Causing sleep.

VIVIAN. Causing sleep.

MR BEARING. Makes you sleepy.

VIVIAN. 'Soporific' means – makes you sleepy – ?

MR BEARING. Correct.

VIVIAN. 'Soporific' means 'makes you sleepy.' Soporific.

MR BEARING. Now use it in a sentence. What has a soporific effect on *you*?

VIVIAN. A soporific effect on me.

MR BEARING. What makes you sleepy?

VIVIAN. Aahh – nothing.

MR BEARING. Correct.

VIVIAN. What about you?

MR BEARING. What has a soporific effect on me? Let me think: boring conversation, I suppose, after dinner.

VIVIAN. Me too, boring conversation.

MR BEARING. Carry on.

VIVIAN. It is said that the effect of eating too much lettuce is soporific.

The little bunnies in the picture are asleep! They're sleeping! Like you said, because of *soporific*!

She stands up, and MR BEARING *exits.*

The illustration bore out the meaning of the word, just as he had explained it. At the time, it seemed like magic.

So imagine the effect that the words of John Donne first had on me: ratiocination, concatenation, coruscation, tergiversation.

Medical terms are less evocative. Still, I want to know what the doctors mean when they . . . anatomise me. And I will grant that in this particular field of endeavour they possess a more potent arsenal of terminology than I. My only defence is the acquisition of vocabulary.

SUSIE *enters and puts her arm around* VIVIAN*'s shoulders to hold her up.* VIVIAN *is shaking, feverish, and weak.*

VIVIAN (*all at once*). Fever and neutropenia.

SUSIE. When did it start?

VIVIAN (*having difficulty speaking*). I – I was at home – reading – and I – felt so bad. I called. Fever and neutropenia. They said to come in.

SUSIE. You did the right thing to come. Did somebody drive you?

VIVIAN. Cab. I took a taxi.

SUSIE (*she grabs a wheelchair and helps* VIVIAN *sit.* As SUSIE *speaks, she takes* VIVIAN*'s temperature, pulse, and respiration rate.*) Here, why don't you sit? Just sit there a minute. I'll get Jason. He's on call tonight. We'll get him to give you some meds. I'm glad I was here on nights. I'll make sure you get to bed soon, okay? It'll just be a minute. I'll get you some juice, some nice juice with lots of ice.

SUSIE *leaves quickly.* VIVIAN *sits there, agitated, confused, and very sick.* SUSIE *returns with the juice.*

VIVIAN. Lights. I left all the lights on at my house.

SUSIE. Don't you worry. It'll be all right.

JASON *enters, roused from his sleep and not fully awake. He wears surgical scrubs and puts on a lab coat as he enters.*

JASON (*without looking at* VIVIAN). How are you feeling, Professor Bearing?

VIVIAN. My teeth – are chattering.

JASON. Vitals.

SUSIE (*giving* VIVIAN *juice and a straw, without looking* at JASON). Temp 39.4. Pulse 120. Respiration 36. Chills and sweating.

JASON. Fever and neutropenia. It's a 'shake and bake'. Blood cultures and urine, stat. Admit her. Prepare for reverse isolation. Start with acetaminophen. Vitals every four hours. (*He starts to leave.*)

SUSIE (*following him*). Jason – I think you need to talk to Kelekian about lowering the dose for the next cycle. It's too much for her like this.

JASON. Lower the dose? No way. Full dose. She's tough. She can take it. Wake me up when the counts come from the lab.

He pads off. SUSIE *wheels* VIVIAN *to her room, and* VIVIAN *collapses on the bed.* SUSIE *connects* VIVIAN*'s IV, then wets a washcloth and rubs her face and neck.* VIVIAN *remains delirious.* SUSIE *checks the IV and leaves with the wheelchair.*

After a while, KELEKIAN *appears in the doorway holding a surgical mask near his face.* JASON *is with him, now dressed and clean-shaven.*

KELEKIAN. Good morning, Dr Bearing. Fifth cycle. Full dose. Definite progress. Everything okay.

VIVIAN (*weakly*). Yes.

KELEKIAN. You're doing swell. Isolation is no problem. Couple of days. Think of it as a vacation.

VIVIAN. Oh.

JASON *starts to enter, holding a mask near his face, just like* KELEKIAN.

KELEKIAN. Jason.

JASON. Oh, Jesus. Okay, okay.

He returns to the doorway, where he puts on a paper gown, mask, and gloves. KELEKIAN *leaves.*

VIVIAN (*to audience*). In isolation, I am isolated. For once I can use a term literally. The chemotherapeutic agents eradicating my cancer have also eradicated my immune system. In my present condition, every living thing is a health hazard to me . . .

JASON *comes in to check the intake-and-output.*

JASON (*complaining to himself*). I really have not got time for this . . .

VIVIAN. . . . particularly health-care professionals.

JASON (*going right to the graph on the wall*). Just to look at the I&0 sheets for one minute, and it takes me half an hour to do precautions. Four, seven, eleven. Two-fifty twice. Okay. (*Remembering.*) Oh, Jeez. Clinical. Professor Bearing. How are you feeling today?

VIVIAN (*very sick*). Fine. Just shaking sometimes from the chills.

JASON. IV will kick in anytime now. No problem. Listen, gotta go. Keep pushing the fluids.

As he exits, he takes off the gown, mask, and gloves.

VIVIAN (*getting up from bed with her IV pole and resuming her explanation*). I am not in isolation because I have cancer, because I have a tumour the size of a grapefruit. No. I am in isolation because I am being treated for cancer. My treatment imperils my health.

Herein lies the paradox. John Donne would revel in it. I would revel in it, if he wrote a poem about it. My students would flounder in it, because paradox is too difficult to understand. Think of it as a puzzle, I would tell them, an intellectual game.

(*She is trapped.*) Or, I *would have* told them. Were it a game. Which it is not.

(*Escaping.*) If they were here, if I were lecturing: How I would *perplex* them! I could work my students into a frenzy. Every ambiguity, every shifting awareness. I could draw so much from the poems.

I could be so powerful.

VIVIAN *stands still, as if conjuring a scene. Now at the height of her powers, she grandly disconnects herself from the IV.* TECHNICIANS *remove the bed and hand her a pointer.*

VIVIAN. The poetry of the early seventeenth century, what has been called the metaphysical school, considers an intractable mental puzzle by exercising the outstanding human faculty of the era, namely *wit.*

The greatest wit – the greatest English poet, some would say – was John Donne. In the Holy Sonnets, Donne applied his capacious, agile wit to the larger aspects of the human experience: life, death, and God.

In his poems, metaphysical quandaries are addressed, but never resolved. Ingenuity, virtuosity, and a vigorous intellect that jousts with the most exalted concepts: these are the tools of wit.

The lights dim. A screen lowers, and the sonnet 'If poysonous mineralls,' from the Gardner edition, appears on it.

VIVIAN *recites.*

If poysonous mineralls, and if that tree,
Whose fruit threw death on else immortall us,
If lecherous goats, if serpents envious
Cannot be damn'd; Alas; why should I bee?
Why should intent or reason, borne in mee,
Make sinnes, else equall, in mee, more heinous?
And mercy being easie, 'and glorious
To God, in his sterne wrath, why threatens hee?
But who am I, that dare dispute with thee?
O God, Oh! of thine onely worthy blood,
And my teares, make a heavenly Lethean flood,
And drowne in it my sinnes blacke memorie.
That thou remember them, some claime as debt,
I thinke it mercy, if thou wilt forget.

VIVIAN *occasionally whacks the screen with a pointer for emphasis. She moves around as she lectures.*

Aggressive intellect. Pious melodrama. And a final, fearful point. Donne's Holy Sonnet Five, 1609. From the Ashford edition, based on Gardner.

The speaker of the sonnet has a brilliant mind, and he plays the part convincingly; but in the end he finds God's *forgiveness* hard to believe, so he crawls under a rock to *hide.*

If arsenic and serpents are not damned, then why is he? In asking the question, the speaker turns eternal damnation into an intellectual game. Why would God choose to do what is *hard,* to condemn, rather than what is *easy,* and also *glorious* – to show mercy?

(Several scholars have disputed Ashford's third comma in line six, but none convincingly.)

But. Exception. Limitation. Contrast. The argument shifts from cleverness to melodrama, an unconvincing eruption of piety: 'O' 'God' 'Oh!'

A typical prayer would plead 'Remember me, O Lord.' (This point is nicely explicated in an article by Richard Strier – a former student of mine who once sat where you do now, although I dare say he was *awake* – in the May 1989 issue of *Modern Philology.*) True believers ask to be *remembered* by God. The speaker of this sonnet asks God to forget. (VIVIAN *moves in front of the screen, and the projection of the poem is cast directly upon her.*) Where is the hyperactive intellect of the first section? Where is the histrionic outpouring of the second? When the speaker considers his own *sins,* and the inevitability of God's *judgement,* he can conceive of but one resolution: to *disappear.* (VIVIAN *moves away from the screen.*) Doctrine assures us that no sinner is denied *forgiveness,* not even one whose sins are overweening *intellect* or overwrought *dramatics.* The speaker does not need to *hide* from God's *judgement,* only to accept God's *forgiveness.* It is very simple. Suspiciously simple.

We want to correct the speaker, to remind him of the assurance of salvation. But it is too late. The poetic encounter is over. We are left to our own consciences. Have we outwitted Donne? Or have we been outwitted?

SUSIE *comes on.*

SUSIE. Ms Bearing?

VIVIAN (*continuing*). Will the po –

SUSIE. Ms Bearing?

VIVIAN (*crossly*). What is it?

SUSIE. You have to go down for a test. Jason just called. They want another ultrasound. They're concerned about a bowel obstruction – Is it okay if I come in?

VIVIAN. No. Not now.

SUSIE. I'm sorry, but they want it now.

VIVIAN. Not right now. It's not *supposed* to be now.

SUSIE. Yes, they want to do it now. I've got the chair.

VIVIAN. It should not be now. I am in the middle of – this. I have *this* planned for now, not ultrasound. No more tests. We've covered that.

SUSIE. I know, I know, but they need for it to be now. It won't take long, and it isn't a bad procedure. Why don't you just come along.

VIVIAN. *I do not want to go now!*

SUSIE. Ms Bearing.

Silence. VIVIAN *raises the screen, walks away from the scene, hooks herself to the IV and gets in the wheelchair* SUSIE *wheels* VIVIAN, *and a* TECHNICIAN *takes her.*

TECHNICIAN. Name.

VIVIAN. B-E-A-R-I-N-G. Kelekian.

TECHNICIAN. It'll just be a minute.

VIVIAN. Time for your break.

TECHNICIAN. Yup. (*The* TECHNICIAN *leaves.*)

VIVIAN (*mordantly*). Take a break!

VIVIAN *sits weakly in the wheelchair.*

VIVIAN.

This is my playes last scene, here heavens appoint
My pilgrimages last mile; and my race
Idly, yet quickly runne, hath this last pace,
My spans last inch, my minutes last point,
And gluttonous death will instantly unjoynt
My body, 'and soule.

John Donne. 1609.

I have always particularly liked that poem. In the abstract. Now I find the image of 'my minute's last point' a little too, shall we say, *pointed.*

I don't mean to complain, but I am becoming very sick. Very, very sick. Ultimately sick, as it were.

In everything I have done, I have been steadfast, resolute – some would say in the extreme. Now, as you can see, I am distinguishing myself in illness.

I have survived eight treatments of Hexamethophosphacil and Vinplatin at the *full* dose, ladies and gentlemen. I have broken the record. I have become something of a celebrity. Kelekian and Jason are simply delighted. I think they foresee celebrity status for themselves upon the appearance of the journal article they will no doubt write about me.

But I flatter myself. The article will not be about *me,* it will be about my ovaries. It will be about my peritoneal cavity, which, despite their best intentions, is now crawling with cancer.

What we have come to think of as *me* is, in fact, just the specimen jar, just the dust jacket, just the white piece of paper that bears the little black marks.

My next line is supposed to be something like this:

'It is such a *relief* to get back to my room after those infernal tests.'

This is hardly true.

It would be a *relief* to be a cheerleader on her way to Daytona Beach for Spring Break.

To get back to my room after those infernal tests is just the next thing that happens.

She returns to her bed, which now has a commode next to it. She is very sick.

Oh, God. It is such a relief to get back to my goddamn room after those goddamn tests.

JASON *enters.*

JASON. Professor Bearing. Just want to check the I&0. Four-fifty, six, five. Okay. How are you feeling today? (*He makes notations on his clipboard throughout the scene.*)

VIVIAN. Fine.

JASON. That's great. just great.

VIVIAN. How are my fluids?

JASON. Pretty good. No kidney involvement yet. That's pretty amazing, with Hex and Vin.

VIVIAN. How will you know when the kidneys are involved?

JASON. Lots of in, not much out.

VIVIAN. That simple.

JASON. Oh, no way. Compromised kidney function is a highly complex reaction. I'm simplifying for you.

VIVIAN. Thank you.

JASON. We're supposed to.

VIVIAN. Bedside manner.

JASON. Yeah, there's a whole course on it in med school. It's required. Colossal waste of time for researchers. (*He turns to go.*)

VIVIAN. I can imagine. (*Trying to ask something important.*) Jason?

JASON. Huh?

VIVIAN (*not sure of herself*). Ah, what . . . (*Quickly.*) What were you just saying?

JASON. When?

VIVIAN. Never mind.

JASON. Professor Bearing?

VIVIAN. Yes.

JASON. Are you experiencing confusion? Short-term memory loss?

VIVIAN. No.

JASON. Sure?

VIVIAN. Yes. (*Pause.*) I was just wondering: why cancer?

JASON. Why cancer?

VIVIAN. Why not open-heart surgery?

JASON. Oh yeah, why not *plumbing.* Why not run a *lube rack,* for all the surgeons know about *Homo sapiens sapiens.* No way. Cancer's the only thing I ever wanted.

VIVIAN (*intrigued*). Huh.

JASON. No, really. Cancer is . . . (*Searching.*)

VIVIAN (*helping*). Awesome.

JASON (*pause*). Yeah. Yeah, that's right. It is. It is awesome. How does it do it? The intercellular regulatory mechanisms – especially for proliferation and differentiation – the malignant neoplasia just don't get it. You grow normal cells in tissue culture in the lab, and they replicate just enough to make a nice, confluent monolayer. They divide twenty times, or fifty times, but eventually they conk out. You grow cancer cells, and they never stop. No contact inhibition whatsoever. They just pile up, just keep replicating forever. (*Pause.*) That's got a funny name. Know what it is?

VIVIAN. No. What?

JASON. Immortality in culture.

VIVIAN. Sounds like a symposium.

JASON. It's an error in judgement, in a molecular way. But *why?* Even on the protistic level the normal cell-cell interactions are so subtle they'll take your breath away. Golden-brown algae, for instance, the lowest multicellular life form on earth – they're *idiots* – and it's incredible. It's perfect. So what's up with the cancer cells? Smartest guys in the world, with the best labs, funding – they don't know what to make of it.

VIVIAN. What about you?

JASON. Me? Oh, I've got a couple of ideas, things I'm kicking around. Wait till I get a lab of my own. If I can survive this . . . *fellowship.*

VIVIAN. The part with the human beings.

JASON. Everybody's got to go through it. All the great researchers. They want us to be able to converse intelligently with the clinicians. As though *researchers* were the impediments. The clinicians are such troglodytes. So smarmy. Like we have to hold hands to discuss creatinine clearance. Just cut the crap, I say.

VIVIAN. Are you going to be sorry when I – Do you ever miss people?

JASON. Everybody asks that. Especially girls.

VIVIAN. What do you tell them?

JASON. I tell them yes.

VIVIAN. Are they persuaded?

JASON. Some.

VIVIAN. Some. I see. (*With great difficulty.*) And what do you say when a patient is . . . apprehensive . . . frightened.

JASON. Of who?

VIVIAN. I just . . . Never mind.

JASON. Professor Bearing, who is the President of the United States?

VIVIAN. I'm fine, really. It's all right.

JASON. You sure? I could order a test –

VIVIAN. No! No, I'm fine. Just a little tired.

JASON. Okay. Look. Gotta go. Keep pushing the fluids. Try for 2,000 a day, okay?

VIVIAN. Okay. To use your word. Okay.

JASON *leaves.*

VIVIAN (*getting out of bed, without her IV*). So. The young doctor, like the senior scholar, prefers research to humanity. At the same time the senior scholar, in her pathetic state as a simpering victim, wishes the young doctor would take more interest in personal contact.

Now I suppose we shall see, through a series of flashbacks, how the senior scholar ruthlessly denied her simpering students the touch of human kindness she now seeks.

STUDENTS *appear sitting at chairs with writing desks attached to the right arm.*

VIVIAN (*commanding attention*). How then would you characterise (*Pointing to a student.*) – you.

STUDENT 1. Huh?

VIVIAN. How would you characterise the animating force of this sonnet?

STUDENT 1. Huh?

VIVIAN. In this sonnet, what is the principal poetic device? I'll give you a hint. It has nothing to do with football. What propels this sonnet?

STUDENT 1. Um.

VIVIAN (*speaking to the audience*). Did I say (*Tenderly.*) 'You are nineteen years old. You are so young. You don't know a sonnet from a steak sandwich.' (*Pause.*) By no means.

(*Sharply, to* STUDENT 1.) You can come to this class prepared, or you can excuse yourself from this class, this department, and this university. Do not think for a moment that I will tolerate anything in between.

(*To the audience, defensively.*) I was teaching him a lesson. (*She walks away from* STUDENT 1, *then turns and addresses the class.*)

So we have another instance of John Donne's agile wit at work: not so much *resolving* the issues of life and God as *revelling* in their complexity.

STUDENT 2. But why?

VIVIAN. Why what?

STUDENT 2. Why does Donne make everything so *complicated?* (*The other* STUDENTS *laugh in agreement.*) No, really, *why?*

VIVIAN (*to the audience*). You know, someone asked me that every year. And it was always one of the smart ones. What could I say? (*To* STUDENT 2.) What do you think?

STUDENT 2. I think it's like he's hiding. I think he's really confused, I don't know, maybe he's scared, so he hides behind all this complicated stuff, hides behind this *wit.*

VIVIAN. *Hides* behind *wit?*

STUDENT 2. I mean, if it's really something he's sure of, he can say it more simple – simply. He doesn't have to be such a brain, or such a performer. It doesn't have to be such a big deal.

The other STUDENTS *encourage him.*

VIVIAN. Perhaps he is suspicious of simplicity.

STUDENT 2. Perhaps, but that's pretty stupid.

VIVIAN (*to the audience*). That observation, despite its infelicitous phrasing, contained the seed of a perspicacious remark. Such an unlikely occurrence left me with two choices. I could draw it out, or I could allow the brain to rest after that heroic effort. If I pursued, there was the chance of great insight, or the risk of undergraduate banality. I could never predict. (*To* STUDENT 2.) Go on.

STUDENT 2. Well, if he's trying to figure out God, and the meaning of life, and big stuff like that, why does he keep running away, you know?

VIVIAN (*to the audience, moving closer to* STUDENT 2). So far so good, but they can think for themselves only so long before they begin to self-destruct.

STUDENT 2. Um, it's like, the more you hide, the less – no, wait – the more you are getting closer – although you don't know it – and the simple thing is there – you see what I mean?

VIVIAN (*to the audience, looking at* STUDENT 2, *as suspense collapses*). Lost it.

(*She walks away and speaks to the audience.*) I distinctly remember an exchange between two students after my lecture on pronunciation and scansion. I overheard them talking on their way out of class. They were young and bright, gathering their books and laughing at the expense of seventeenth-century poetry, at my expense.

(*To the class*) To scan the line properly, we must take advantage of the contemporary flexibility in 'i-o-n' endings, as in 'expansion.' The quatrain stands:

> Our two souls therefore, which are one,
>   Though I must go, endure not yet
> A breach, but an ex-*pan*-see-on,
>   Like gold to airy thinness beat.

Bear this in mind in your reading. That's all for today.

The STUDENTS *get up in a chaotic burst.* STUDENT 3 *and* STUDENT 4 *pass by* VIVIAN *on their way out.*

STUDENT 3. I hope I can get used to this pronuncia-see-on.

STUDENT 4. I know. I hope I can survive this course and make it to gradua-see-on.

They laugh. VIVIAN *glowers at them. They fall silent, embarrassed.*

VIVIAN (*to the audience*). That was a witty little exchange, I must admit. It showed the mental acuity I would praise in a poetic text. But I admired only the studied application of wit, not its spontaneous eruption.

STUDENT 1 *interrupts.*

STUDENT 1. Professor Bearing? Can I talk to you for a minute?

VIVIAN. You may.

STUDENT 1. I need to ask for an extension on my paper. I'm really sorry, and I know your policy, but see –

VIVIAN. Don't tell me. Your grandmother died.

STUDENT 1. You knew.

VIVIAN. It was a guess.

STUDENT 1. I have to go home.

VIVIAN. Do what you will, but the paper is due when it is due.

As STUDENT 1 *leaves and the classroom disappears,* VIVIAN *watches. Pause.*

VIVIAN. I don't know. I feel so much – what is the word? I look back, I see these scenes, and I . . .

Long silence. VIVIAN *walks absently around the stage, trying to think of something. Finally, giving up, she trudges back to bed.*

VIVIAN. It was late at night, the graveyard shift. Susie was on. I could hear her in the hall.

I wanted her to come and see me. So I had to create a little emergency. Nothing dramatic.

VIVIAN *pinches the IV tubing. The pump alarm beeps.*

It worked.

SUSIE *enters, concerned.*

SUSIE. Ms Bearing? Is that you beeping at four in the morning? (*She checks the tubing and presses buttons on the pump. The alarm stops.*) Did that wake you up? I'm sorry. It just gets occluded sometimes.

VIVIAN. I was awake.

SUSIE. You were? What's the trouble, sweetheart?

VIVIAN (*to the audience, roused*). Do not think for a minute that anyone calls me 'Sweetheart'. But then . . . I allowed it. (*To* SUSIE.) Oh, I don't know.

SUSIE. You can't sleep?

VIVIAN. No. I just keep thinking.

SUSIE. If you do that too much, you can get kind of confused.

VIVIAN. I know. I can't figure things out. I'm in a . . . *quandary,* having these . . . *doubts.*

SUSIE. What you're doing is very hard.

VIVIAN. Hard things are what I like best.

SUSIE. It's not the same. It's like it's out of control, isn't it?

VIVIAN (*crying, in spite of herself*). I'm scared.

SUSIE (*stroking her*). Oh, honey, of course you are.

VIVIAN. I want . . .

SUSIE. I know. It's hard.

VIVIAN. I don't feel sure of myself any more.

SUSIE. And you used to feel sure.

VIVIAN (*crying*). Oh, yes, I used to feel sure.

SUSIE. Vivian. It's all right. I know. It hurts. I know. It's all right. Do you want a tissue? It's all right. (*Silence.*) Vivian, would you like a Popsicle?

VIVIAN (*like a child*). Yes, please.

SUSIE. I'll get it for you. I'll be right back.

VIVIAN. Thank you.

SUSIE *leaves.*

VIVIAN (*pulling herself together*). The epithelial cells in my GI tract have been killed by the chemo. The cold Popsicle feels good, it's something I can digest, and it helps keep me hydrated. For your information.

SUSIE *returns with an orange two-stick Popsicle.* VIVIAN *unwraps it and breaks it in half.*

VIVIAN. Here.

SUSIE. Sure?

VIVIAN. Yes.

SUSIE. Thanks. (SUSIE *sits on the commode by the bed. Silence.*) When I was a kid, we used to get these from a truck. The man would come around and ring his bell and we'd all run over. Then we'd sit on the curb and eat our Popsicles.

Pretty profound, huh?

VIVIAN. It sounds nice.

Silence.

SUSIE. Vivian, there's something we need to talk about, you need to think about.

Silence.

VIVIAN. My cancer is not being cured, is it.

SUSIE. Huh-uh.

VIVIAN. They never expected it to be, did they.

SUSIE. Well, they thought the drugs would make the tumour get smaller, and it has gotten a lot smaller. But the problem is that it started in new places too. They've learned a lot for their research. It was the best thing they had to give you, the strongest drugs. There just isn't a good treatment for what you have yet, for advanced ovarian. I'm sorry. They should have explained this –

VIVIAN. I knew.

SUSIE. You did.

VIVIAN. I read between the lines.

SUSIE. What you have to think about is your 'code status.' What you want them to do if your heart stops.

VIVIAN. Well.

SUSIE. You can be 'full code,' which means that if your heart stops, they'll call a Code Blue and the code team will come and resuscitate you and take you to Intensive Care until you stabilise again. Or you can be 'Do Not Resuscitate', so if your heart stops we'll . . . well, we'll just let it. You'll be 'DNR'. You can think about it, but I wanted to present both choices before Kelekian and Jason talk to you.

VIVIAN. You don't agree about this?

SUSIE. Well, they like to save lives. So anything's okay, as long as life continues. It doesn't matter if you're hooked up to a million machines. Kelekian is a great researcher and everything. And the fellows, like Jason, they're really smart. it's really an honour for them to work with him. But they always . . . want to know more things.

VIVIAN. I always want to know more things. I'm a scholar. Or I was when I had shoes, when I had eyebrows.

SUSIE. Well, okay then. You'll be full code. That's fine.

Silence.

VIVIAN. No, don't complicate the matter.

SUSIE. It's okay. It's up to you –

VIVIAN. Let it stop.

SUSIE. Really?

VIVIAN. Yes.

SUSIE. So if your heart stops beating –

VIVIAN. Just let it stop.

SUSIE. Sure?

VIVIAN. Yes.

SUSIE. Okay. I'll get Kelekian to give the order, and then –

VIVIAN. Susie?

SUSIE. Uh-huh?

VIVIAN. You're still going to take care of me, aren't you?

SUSIE. 'Course, sweetheart. Don't you worry.

As SUSIE *leaves,* VIVIAN *sits upright, full of energy and rage.*

VIVIAN. That certainly was a *maudlin* display. Popsicles? 'Sweetheart?' I can't believe my life has become so . . . *corny.*

But it can't be helped. I don't see any other way. We are discussing life and death, and not in the abstract, either; we are discussing *my* life and *my* death, and my brain is dulling, and poor Susie's was never very sharp to begin with, and I can't conceive of any other . . . *tone.*

(*Quickly.*) Now is not the time for verbal swordplay, for unlikely flights of imagination and wildly shifting perspectives, for metaphysical conceit, for wit.

And nothing would be worse than a detailed scholarly analysis. Erudition. Interpretation. Complication.

(*Slowly.*) Now is a time for simplicity. Now is a time for, dare I say it, kindness.

(*Searchingly.*) I thought being extremely smart would take care of it. But I see that I have been found out. Ooohhh.

I'm scared. Oh, God. I want . . . I want . . . No. I want to hide. I just want to curl up in a little ball. (*She dives under the covers.*)

VIVIAN *wakes in horrible pain. She is tense, agitated, fearful. Slowly she calms down and addresses the audience.*

VIVIAN (*trying extremely hard*). I want to tell you how it feels. I want to explain it, to use *my* words. It's as if . . . I can't . . . There aren't . . . I'm like a student and this is the final exam and I don't know what to put down because I don't understand the question and I'm *running out of time.*

The time for extreme measures has come. I am in terrible pain. Susie says that I need to begin aggressive pain management if I am going to stand it.

'It': such a little word. In this case, I think 'it' signifies 'being alive'.

I apologise in advance for what this palliative treatment modality does to the dramatic coherence of my play's last scene. It can't be helped. They have to do something. I'm in terrible pain.

Say it, Vivian. *It hurts like hell. It really does.*

SUSIE *enters.* VIVIAN *is writhing in pain.*

Oh, God. Oh, God.

SUSIE. Sshh. It's okay. Sshh. I paged Kelekian up here, and we'll get you some meds.

VIVIAN. Oh, God, it is so painful. So painful. So much pain. So much pain.

SUSIE. I know, I know, it's okay. Sshh, just try and clear your mind. It's all right. We'll get you a Patient-Controlled Analgesic. It's a little pump, and you push a little button, and you decide how much medication you want. (*Importantly.*) It's very simple, and it's up to you.

KELEKIAN *storms in;* JASON *follows with chart.*

KELEKIAN. Dr Bearing. Susie.

SUSIE. Time for Patient-Controlled Analgesic. The pain is killing her.

KELEKIAN. Dr Bearing, are you in pain? (KELEKIAN *holds out his hand for chart;* JASON *hands it to him. They read.*)

VIVIAN (*sitting up, unnoticed by the staff*). Am I in pain?
I don't believe this. Yes, I'm in goddamn pain. (*Furious.*)
I have a fever of 101 spiking to 104. And I have bone
metastases in my pelvis and both femurs. (*Screaming.*)
There is cancer eating away at my goddamn bones, and
I did not know there could be such pain on this earth.

(*She flops back on the bed and cries audibly to them.*) Oh, God.

KELEKIAN (*looking at* VIVIAN *intently*). I want a morphine drip.

SUSIE. What about Patient-Controlled? She could be more alert –

KELEKIAN (*teaching*). Ordinarily, yes. But in her case, no.

SUSIE. But –

KELEKIAN (*to* SUSIE). She's earned a rest. (*To* JASON.) Morphine, ten push now, then start at ten an hour. (*To* VIVIAN.) Dr Bearing, try to relax. We're going to help you through this, don't worry. Dr Bearing? Excellent. (*He squeezes* VIVIAN*'s shoulder. They all leave.*)

VIVIAN (*weakly, painfully, leaning on her IV pole, she moves to address the audience*). Hi. How are you feeling today?

Silence.

These are my last coherent lines. I'll have to leave the action to the professionals.

It came so quickly, after taking so long. Not even time for a proper conclusion.

VIVIAN *concentrates with all her might, and she attempts a grand summation, as if trying to conjure her own ending.*

> And Death – *capital D* – shall be no more – *semi-colon.*
> Death – *capital D* – thou shalt die – *ex-cla-mation point!*

She looks down at herself, looks out at the audience, and sees that the line doesn't work. She shakes her head and exhales with resignation.

I'm sorry.

She gets back into bed as SUSIE *injects morphine into the IV tubing.* VIVIAN *lies down and, in a final melodramatic gesture, shuts the lids of her own eyes and folds her arms over her chest.*

VIVIAN. I trust this will have a soporific effect.

SUSIE. Well, I don't know about that, but it sure makes you sleepy.

This strikes VIVIAN *as delightfully funny. She starts to giggle, then laughs out loud.* SUSIE *doesn't get it.*

SUSIE. What's so funny? (VIVIAN *keeps laughing.*) What?

VIVIAN. Oh! it's that – 'Soporific' – *means* 'makes you sleepy'.

SUSIE. It does?

VIVIAN. Yes. (*Another fit of laughter.*)

SUSIE (*giggling*). Well, that was pretty dumb –

VIVIAN. No! No, no! It was *funny!*

SUSIE (*starting to catch on*). Yeah, I guess so. (*Laughing.*) In a dumb sort of way. (*This sets them both off laughing again.*) I never would have gotten it. I'm glad you explained it.

VIVIAN (*simply*). I'm a teacher.

They laugh a little together Slowly the morphine kicks in, and VIVIAN*'s laughs become long sighs. Finally she falls asleep.* SUSIE *checks everything out, then leaves. Long silence.*

JASON *and* SUSIE *chat as they enter to insert a catheter.*

JASON. Oh, yeah. She was a great scholar. Wrote tons of books, articles, was the head of everything. (*He checks the I&0 sheet.*) Two hundred. Seventy-five. Five-twenty. Let's up the hydration. She won't be drinking any more. See if we can keep her kidneys from fading. Yeah, I had a lot of respect for her, which is more than I can say for the *entire* biochemistry department.

SUSIE. What do you want? Dextrose?

JASON. Give her saline.

SUSIE. Okay.

JASON. She gave a hell of a lecture. No notes, not a word out of place. It was pretty impressive. A lot of students hated her, though.

SUSIE. Why?

JASON. Well, she wasn't exactly a cupcake.

SUSIE (*laughing, fondly*). Well, she hasn't exactly been a cupcake here, either. (*Leaning over* VIVIAN *and talking loudly and slowly in her ear.*) Now, Ms Bearing, Jason and I are here, and we're going to insert a catheter to collect your urine. It's not going to hurt, don't you worry. (*During the conversation she inserts the catheter.*)

JASON. Like she can hear you.

SUSIE. It's just nice to do.

JASON. Eight cycles of Hex and Vin at the full dose. Kelekian didn't think it was possible. I wish they could all get through it at full throttle. Then we could really have some data.

SUSIE. She's not what I imagined. I thought somebody who studied poetry would be sort of dreamy, you know?

JASON. Oh, not the way she did it. It felt more like boot camp than English class. This guy John Donne was incredibly intense. Like your whole brain had to be in knots before you could get it.

SUSIE. He made it hard on purpose?

JASON. Well, it has to do with the subject. The Holy Sonnets we worked on most, they were mostly about Salvation Anxiety. That's a term I made up in one of my papers, but I think it fits pretty well. Salvation Anxiety. You're this brilliant guy, I mean, brilliant – this guy makes Shakespeare sound like a Hallmark card. And you know you're a sinner. And there's this promise of salvation, the whole religious thing. But you just can't deal with it.

SUSIE. How come?

JASON. It just doesn't stand up to scrutiny. But you can't face life without it either. So you write these screwed-up sonnets. Everything is brilliantly convoluted. Really tricky stuff. Bouncing off the walls. Like a game, to make the puzzle so complicated.

The catheter is inserted. SUSIE *puts things away.*

SUSIE. But what happens in the end?

JASON. End of what?

SUSIE. To John Donne. Does he ever get it?

JASON. Get what?

SUSIE. His Salvation Anxiety. Does he ever understand?

JASON. Oh, no way. The puzzle takes over. You're not even trying to solve it any more. Fascinating, really. Great training for lab research. Looking at things in increasing levels of complexity.

SUSIE. Until what?

JASON. What do you mean?

SUSIE. Where does it end? Don't you get to solve the puzzle?

JASON. Nah. When it comes right down to it, research is just trying to quantify the complications of the puzzle.

SUSIE. But you *help* people! You save lives and stuff.

JASON. Oh, yeah, I save some guy's life, and then the poor slob gets hit by a bus!

SUSIE (*confused*). Yeah, I guess so. I just don't think of it that way. Guess you can tell I never took a class in poetry.

JASON. Listen, if there's one thing we learned in Seventeenth-Century Poetry, it's that you can forget about that sentimental stuff. *Enzyme Kinetics* was more poetic than Bearing's class. Besides, you can't think about that *meaning-of-life* garbage all the time or you'd go nuts.

SUSIE. Do you believe in it?

JASON. In what?

SUSIE. Umm. I don't know, the meaning-of-life garbage. (*She laughs a little.*)

JASON. What do they *teach* you in nursing school? (*Checking* VIVIAN*'s pulse.*) She's out of it. Shouldn't be too long. You done here?

SUSIE. Yeah, I'll just . . . tidy up.

JASON. See ya. (*He leaves.*)

SUSIE. Bye, Jace. (*She thinks for a minute, then carefully rubs baby oil on* VIVIAN*'s hands. She checks the catheter, then leaves.*)

PROFESSOR E. M. ASHFORD*, now eighty, enters.*

E.M. Vivian? Vivian? It's Evelyn. Vivian?

VIVIAN (*waking, slurred*). Oh, God. (*Surprised.*) Professor Ashford. Oh, God.

E.M. I'm in town visiting my great-grandson, who is celebrating his fifth birthday. I went to see you at your office, and they directed me here. (*She lays her jacket, scarf and parcel on the bed.*) I have been walking all over town. I had forgotten how early it gets chilly here.

VIVIAN (*weakly*). I feel so bad.

E.M. I know you do. I can see. (VIVIAN *cries.*) Oh, dear, there, there. There, there. (VIVIAN *cries more, letting the tears flow.*) Vivian, Vivian.

(E.M. *looks toward the hall, then furtively slips off her shoes and swings up on the bed. She puts her arm around* VIVIAN.) There, there. There, there, Vivian. (*Silence.*)

It's a windy day. (*Silence.*)

Don't worry, dear. (*Silence.*)

Let's see. Shall I recite to you? Would you like that? I'll recite something by Donne.

VIVIAN (*moaning*). Nooooooo.

E.M. Very well. (*Silence.*) Hmmm. (*Silence.*) Little Jeffrey is very sweet. Gets into everything.

Silence. E.M. *takes a children's book out of the paper bag and begins reading.* VIVIAN *nestles in, drifting in and out of sleep.*

Let's see. *The Runaway Bunny.* By Margaret Wise Brown. Pictures by Clement Hurd. Copyright 1942. First Harper Trophy Edition, 1972.

Now then.

Once there was a little bunny who wanted to run away.

So he said to his mother, 'I am running away.'

'If you run away,' said his mother, 'I will run after you. For you are my little bunny.'

'If you run after me,' said the little bunny, 'I will become a fish in a trout stream and I will swim away from you.'

'If you become a fish in a trout stream,' said his mother, 'I will become a fisherman and I will fish for you.'

(*Thinking out loud.*) Look at that. A little allegory of the soul. No matter where it hides, God will find it. See, Vivian?

VIVIAN (*moaning*). Uhhhhhh.

E.M. 'If you become a fisherman,' said the little bunny, 'I will be a bird and fly away from you.'

'If you become a bird and fly away from me,' said his mother, 'I will be a tree that you come home to.'

(*To herself.*) Very clever.

'Shucks,' said the little bunny, 'I might just as well stay where I am and be your little bunny.'

And so he did. 'Have a carrot,' said the mother bunny.

(*To herself.*) Wonderful.

VIVIAN *is now fast asleep.* E.M. *slowly gets down and gathers her things. She leans over and kisses her.*

It's time to go. And flights of angels sing thee to thy rest. (*She leaves.*)

JASON *strides in and goes directly to the I&0 sheet without looking at* VIVIAN.

JASON. Professor Bearing. How are you feeling today? Three p.m. IV hydration totals. Two thousand in. Thirty out. Uh-oh. That's it. Kidneys gone.

(*He looks at* VIVIAN.) Professor Bearing? Highly unresponsive. Wait a second – (*Puts his head down to her mouth and chest to listen for heartbeat and breathing.*) Wait a sec – Jesus Christ! (*Yelling.*) CALL A CODE!

JASON throws down the chart, dives over the bed, and lies on top of her body as he reaches for the phone and punches in the numbers.

(*To himself.*) Code: 4-5-7-5. (*To operator.*) Code Blue, room 707. Code Blue, room 707. Dr Posner – P-O-S-N-E-R. Hurry up!

He throws down the phone and lowers the head of the bed.

Come on, come on, COME ON.

He begins CPR, kneeling over VIVIAN, *alternately pounding frantically and giving mouth-to-mouth resuscitation.*

Over the loudspeaker in the hall, a droning voice repeats 'Code Blue, room 707. Code Blue, room 707.'

One! Two! Three! Four! Five! (*He breathes in her mouth.*)

SUSIE, *hearing the announcement, runs into the room.*

SUSIE. WHAT ARE YOU DOING?

JASON. A GODDAMN CODE. GET OVER HERE!

SUSIE. She's DNR! (*She grabs him.*)

JASON (*he pushes her away*). She's Research!

SUSIE. She's NO CODE!

SUSIE *grabs* JASON *and hurls him off the bed.*

JASON. Ooowww! Goddamnit, Susie!

SUSIE. She's no code!

JASON. Aaargh!

SUSIE. Kelekian put the order in – you saw it! You were right there, Jason! Oh, God, the code! (*She runs to the phone. He struggles to stand.*) 4-5-7-5.

The CODE TEAM *swoops in. Everything changes. Frenzy takes over. They knock* SUSIE *out of the way with their equipment.*

SUSIE (*at the phone*). Cancel code, room 707. Sue Monahan, primary nurse. Cancel code. Dr Posner is here.

JASON (*in agony*). Oh, God.

CODE TEAM.
– Get out of the way!
– Unit staff out!
– Get the board!
– Over here!

They throw VIVIAN*'s body up at the waist and stick a board underneath for CPR. In a whirlwind of sterile packaging and barked commands, one team member attaches a respirator, one begins CPR, and one prepares the defibrillator.* SUSIE *and* JASON *try to stop them but are pushed away.*

The loudspeaker in the hall announces 'Cancel code, room 707. Cancel code, room 707.'

CODE TEAM.
– Bicarb amp!
– I got it! (*To* SUSIE.) Get out!
– One, two, three, four, five!
– Get ready to shock! (*To* JASON.) Move it!

SUSIE (*running to each person, yelling*). STOP! Patient is DNR!

JASON (*at the same time, to the* CODE TEAM). No, no! Stop doing this. STOP!

CODE TEAM.
– Keep it going!
– What do you get?
– Bicarb amp!
– No pulse!

SUSIE. She's NO CODE! Order was given – (*She dives for the chart and holds, it up as she cries out.*) Look! Look at this! DO NOT RESUSCITATE. KELEKIAN.

CODE TEAM (*as they administer electric shock,* VIVIAN*'s body arches and bounces back down*).
– Almost ready!
– Hit her!
– CLEAR!
– Pulse? Pulse?

JASON (*howling*). I MADE A MISTAKE!

Pause. The CODE TEAM *looks at him. He collapses on the floor.*

SUSIE. No code! Patient is no code.

CODE TEAM HEAD. Who the hell are you?

SUSIE. Sue Monahan, primary nurse.

CODE TEAM HEAD. Let me see the goddamn chart. CHART!

CODE TEAM (*slowing down*).
– What's going on?
– Should we stop?
– What's it say?

SUSIE (*pushing them away from the bed*). Patient is no code. Get away from her!

SUSIE *lifts the blanket.* VIVIAN *steps out of the bed.*

CODE TEAM HEAD (*reading*). Do Not Resuscitate. Kelekian. Shit.

She walks away from the scene, toward a little light.

The CODE TEAM *stops working.*

She is now attentive and eager, moving slowly toward the light.

JASON (*whispering*). Oh, God.

CODE TEAM HEAD. Order was put in yesterday.

She takes off her cap and lets it drop.

She slips off her bracelet.

CODE TEAM.
– It's a doctor fuck up.

She loosens the ties and the top gown slides to the floor.

– What is he, a resident?

She lets the second gown fall.

– Got us up here on a DNR.
– Called a code on a no-code.

The instant she is naked, and beautiful, reaching for the light –

JASON. Oh, God.

The bedside scene fades.

Lights out.